Rhode Island

Niels R. Jensen

Visit us at
www.abdopublishing.com

Published by ABDO Publishing Company, 8000 West 78th Street, Suite 310, Edina, Minnesota 55439 USA. Copyright ©2010 by Abdo Consulting Group, Inc. International copyrights reserved in all countries. No part of this book may be reproduced in any form without written permission from the publisher. The Checkerboard Library™ is a trademark and logo of ABDO Publishing Company.

Printed in the United States.

Editor: John Hamilton
Graphic Design: Sue Hamilton
Cover Illustration: Neil Klinepier
Cover Photo: iStock Photo
Interior Photo Credits: Alamy, AP Images, Corbis, Getty, Granger Collection, iStock Photo, Jupiterimages, Library of Congress, Marc N. Belanger, Michelle St.Sauveur, Mile High Maps, Mountain High Maps, NASA/GSFC-Jeff Schmaltz/MODIS Rapid Response Team, NOAA/C. Flagg, One Mile Up, Photo Researchers, Rhode Island National Guard, and the University of Wisconsin-Milwaukee/Adriaen Block Chart.
Statistics: State population statistics taken from 2008 U.S. Census Bureau estimates. City and town population statistics taken from July 1, 2007, U.S. Census Bureau estimates. Land and water area statistics taken from 2000 Census, U.S. Census Bureau.

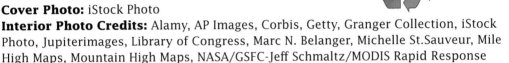

Manufactured with paper containing at least 10% post-consumer waste

Library of Congress Cataloging-in-Publication Data

Jensen, Niels R., 1949-
  Rhode Island / Niels R. Jensen.
      p. cm. -- (The United States)
  Includes index.
  ISBN 978-1-60453-675-1
  1. Rhode Island--Juvenile literature. I. Title.

F79.3.J46 2010
974.5--dc22
                                    2008052399

Table of Contents

The Ocean State

Rhode Island is the smallest state of the United States. However, it is very densely populated. It is a compact powerhouse, with one of the best economies in the nation for its size.

Rhode Island is part of New England, on the East Coast. It is one of the original 13 colonies. It grew as a colony because people found religious freedom there.

Rhode Island is nicknamed the Ocean State. It has more than 400 miles (644 km) of coastline along the Atlantic Ocean. People come to Rhode Island to sail its waters, and relax on the sandy beaches. There are many interesting and beautiful things to see for both visitors and residents.

Completed in 1890, Castle Hill Lighthouse stands near Newport, Rhode Island. It still operates today, assisting ships entering Narragansett Bay.

Quick Facts

Name: Origin uncertain. Dutch explorer Adriaen Block called Rhode Island the Roodt Eylandt (Red Island). Another early explorer, Giovanni de Verrazzano, said Block Island reminded him of the Greek island of Rhodes.

State Capital: Providence

Date of Statehood: May 29, 1790 (13th state)

Population: 1,050,788 (43rd-most populous state)

Area (Total Land and Water): 1,214 square miles (3,144 sq km), smallest state

Largest City: Providence, population 172,459

Nickname: The Ocean State

Motto: Hope

State Bird: Rhode Island Red Chicken

Violet

Cumberlandite

Red Maple

Jerimoth Hill

Atlantic Ocean

State Flower: Violet

State Rock: Cumberlandite

State Tree: Red Maple

State Song: "Rhode Island's It For Me"

Highest Point: 812 feet (247 m), Jerimoth Hill

Lowest Point: 0 ft. (0 m), Atlantic Ocean

Average July Temperature: 70°F (21°C)

Record High Temperature: 104°F (40°C) in Providence, August 2, 1975

Average January Temperature: 29°F (-2°C)

Record Low Temperature: -25°F (-32°C) in Greene, February 6, 1996

Average Annual Precipitation: 44 inches (112 cm)

Number of U.S. Senators: 2

Number of U.S. Representatives: 2

U.S. Postal Service Abbreviation: RI

Geography

Rhode Island is the smallest state. It covers just 1,214 square miles (3,144 sq km). However, its coastline is 400 miles (644) long.

The state is fairly flat, and has good farmland. The highest point is Jerimoth Hill, by the Connecticut border. It is 812 feet (247 m) above sea level.

There are two main geographical regions in Rhode Island. The western two-thirds of the state is upland. There are rolling hills, forests, lakes, ponds, streams, and rivers. This area is part of the Appalachian Mountains. They were pushed up more than 400 million years ago when the huge continental plates came together.

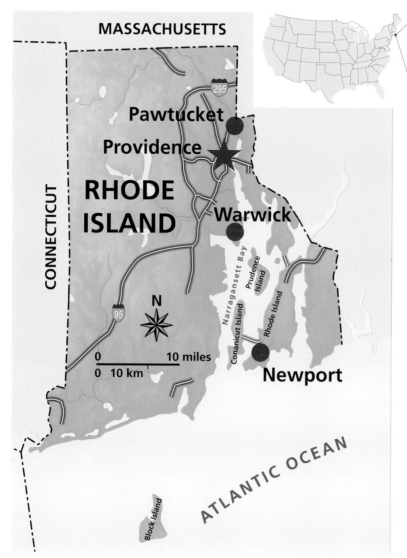

MASSACHUSETTS

CONNECTICUT

Pawtucket

Providence

RHODE ISLAND

Warwick

Narragansett Bay

Prudence Island

Conanicut Island

Rhode Island

N

0   10 miles
0   10 km

Newport

ATLANTIC OCEAN

Block Island

Rhode Island's total land and water area is 1,214 square miles (3,144 sq km). It is the smallest state. The state capital is Providence.

The eastern third of the state is coastal lowland. It includes Narragansett Bay. There are sandy beaches, salt marshes, and lagoons. The Pawtuxet, Blackstone, and Providence Rivers flow through there.

Narragansett Bay is New England's largest estuary. It has more than 30 islands.

A satellite image of New England.

The three largest are Aquidneck, Conanicut, and Prudence. It is Aquidneck Island that the Dutch explorer Adriaen Block called Roodt Eylandt (Red Island). It is officially named Rhode Island, but it is commonly called Aquidneck Island to avoid confusion with the state as a whole.

Block Island is 12 miles (19 km) from the mainland. It is a moraine that was left by ice age glaciers. All of Rhode Island was once covered by ice one-mile (1.6-km) thick during the last ice age. As the glaciers moved, they scraped and shaped the land under them. When they melted, they left behind sand, gravel, and other deposits. The last glacier melted about 10,000 years ago.

Southeast Light sits on a rocky point of Block Island.

Climate and Weather

Rhode Island has a humid continental climate. It is wet and changeable, with large swings in daily and seasonal temperatures.

There are four distinct seasons in the state. Summers are hot and rainy. Winters are cold and snowy. The sea affects the coastal areas, such as Narragansett Bay and Block Island. They are cooler in summer, and warmer in winter, than the rest of the state.

A man shovels during a snowstorm in Providence, Rhode Island.

The state has thunderstorms and blizzards. Hurricanes also sometimes hit Rhode Island. They have whipped up storm surges up to 18 feet (5 m) high. The result can be widespread damage and loss of life along the coast. Some of the state's worst storms included the Great Gale of 1815, the Hurricane of 1938, and 1954's Hurricane Carol.

The Edgewood Yacht Club in Rhode Island is submerged by Hurricane Carol's storm surge in 1954.

The Hurricane of 1938 caused buildings to be completely washed away and widespread flooding in Providence, Rhode Island.

Plants and Animals

About 60 percent of Rhode Island is forest. In the fall, visitors come to see the leaves turn colors from green to bright red, yellow, and orange. When the leaves die, their green pigment fades away, while the other color pigments remain.

The state's trees include ash, birch, cedar, oak, hickory, pine, tulip tree, and many others. Some trees are used for timber products, and some for firewood. Christmas trees are commercially grown in the state. The official state tree is the red maple.

The coastal salt marshes and ponds are very special environments. Besides their natural beauty, they are habitat for hundreds of species of birds, animals, plants, and fish.

Hundreds of monarch butterflies rest on a tree in Rhode Island.

The state has beavers, bobcats, coyotes, deer, fishers, foxes, muskrats, opossums, otters, raccoons, rabbits, skunks, weasels, and woodcocks.

Rhode Island is a wonderful place for bird watchers. There are doves, ducks, eagles, egrets, falcons, geese, gulls, herons, loons, pheasants, ruffed grouses, sparrows, swans, wild turkeys, and many others. A large number of migrating birds pass through the state.

Rhode Island's saltwater and freshwater fish include bass, bluefish, flounder, menhaden, pickerel, pollock, scup, swordfish, tautog, trout and weakfish. Clams, crabs, lobsters, oysters, and mussels are common shellfish. There are huge finback and humpback whales in the ocean, as well as dolphins, seals, and sea turtles.

Lobster

A great black-backed gull with a spider crab.

Snapping Turtle

Harbor Seal

Woodcock

History

Before Europeans settled the Rhode Island area, Native Americans hunted, fished, and grew crops. They included the Wampanoag, Pequot, Narragansett, and Nipmuck peoples.

In 1524, Italian Giovanni de Verrazzano explored what is now called Block Island and Narragansett Bay. Dutchman Adriaen Block and Englishman John Smith made separate explorations of the area in 1614.

The first permanent settlement of the area was built in 1636. Roger Williams had been banished from Massachusetts for religious reasons. He bought land from the Narragansett Native Americans. He founded the city of Providence, and established religious and political freedoms.

In 1636, Roger Williams came to Rhode Island, bought land from the Narragansett tribe, and founded the city of Providence.

Others soon followed Roger Williams. Pioneer and minister Ann Hutchinson and her followers founded Portsmouth in 1638. Newport, Warwick, Wickford, and Pawtuxet were built shortly afterwards.

In 1663, the area became an official colony of Great Britain. Tensions grew between the English colonists and Native Americans. In 1675, a two-year war broke out called King Philip's War. There was much suffering and death on both sides. The colonists eventually won.

King Philip, also known as Metacomet, chief of the Wampanoags, led the war against the American colonists. Many people died before the war ended in 1676.

Starting in the mid-1600s, Rhode Island's wealth was tied to ocean trade. The colonists were active in shipping and privateering. There were also pirates. Newport and Bristol became major slave markets.

As time passed, British taxes and rules angered the people of Rhode Island. The first blood of the American Revolution was spilled here in 1772, when patriots burned the English ship HMS *Gaspee*.

In 1772, the British schooner *Gaspee* was burned by American patriots in Narragansett Bay.

During the Revolutionary War (1775-1783), British forces occupied Newport, Rhode Island. Even so, Rhode Island troops fought in the war's major battles.

After the war, Rhode Island was the last to approve, or ratify, the United States Constitution. It became the 13th state on May 29, 1790.

In the late 1700s, America's Industrial Revolution began. Many Rhode Island towns became major manufacturing centers. People moved into the state to find work.

Rhode Island outlawed the slave trade in 1787. Thousands of people used the Underground Railroad to get to freedom.

Rhode Island sent more than 25,000 men to fight in the Civil War (1861-1865). Rhode Island's factories produced bullets, canons, guns, and other war materials.

Civil War officers of the 1st Rhode Island Volunteers of 1861. The sign welcomes their commander, Colonel Burnside.

Built in Pawtucket in 1793, Samuel Slater's Mill was one of the first cotton mills in the United States.

After the Civil War, industry kept growing. Rhode Island factories made products such as cotton, wool, metal parts, and steam engines.

In the first half of the 1900s, Rhode Island companies made many supplies for America's involvement in World War I and World War II. But in the second half of the century, manufacturing became less important. Many factories closed, or moved to other states. Tourism and service jobs became more important to Rhode Island. Today, government and health care are the leading employers.

Did You Know?

- Rhode Island has the world's largest termite. The big blue bug is 58 feet (18 m) long. It sits on top of Providence's New England Pest Control building.

- Several Rhode Island ship owners received privateering licenses from the government. Some unfortunately turned to piracy, and the colony was accused of sheltering criminals. On July 19, 1723, 26 pirates were hanged at Gravelly Point in the city of Newport.

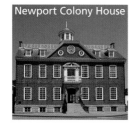

Newport Colony House

- Rhode Island had two state capitals until 1900. The legislature switched

its sessions between Providence and Newport. All sessions are now at the state house in Providence.

- The First Rhode Island Regiment was a Continental army unit during the Revolutionary War. It was one of the nation's first military units to include African American soldiers. The regiment stopped three British assaults at the Battle of Rhode Island in 1778. It also helped at the siege of Yorktown in 1781.

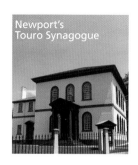

Newport's Touro Synagogue

- Religious freedom made Rhode Island a haven for Baptists, Quakers, Huguenots, and Jews. Newport's Touro Synagogue is the oldest surviving Jewish synagogue in the U.S. It was dedicated in 1763.

People

George M. Cohan (1878-1942) is called the father of the American musical comedy. He produced many popular Broadway plays. He was a talented actor, composer, dancer, director, entertainer, lyricist, playwright, and singer. His songs include "The Yankee Doodle Boy" and "Give My Regards to Broadway." Cohan was born in Providence.

Meredith Vieira

(1953-) is a journalist and television co-host of NBC's *Today*. She is also a host of the game show *Who Wants to Be a Millionaire*. She is a former host of *The View*, and also worked as a correspondent on the CBS news show *60 Minutes*. Vieira was born in East Providence.

Nathanael Greene (1742–1786) was a major general during the American Revolution. He was a skilled soldier, and a close friend of George Washington. Green's war-planning skill was a serious blow to the British. He was born in Warwick.

Matthew Perry (1794–1858) was a commodore of the United States Navy. He was sent by President Millard Fillmore to establish trade with Japan. In 1854, he signed the Kanagawa Treaty, ending Japan's isolation. He was born in South Kingston.

Gilbert Stuart (1755-1828) was one of America's greatest portrait artists. He painted the picture of George Washington that is printed on the one-dollar bill. He made portraits of more than 1,000 people, including 6 presidents. Stuart was born in Saunderstown.

Vinny "Paz" Pazienza (1962-) is a former five-time world champion boxer. He won his first title fight in 1987. He fought under the nickname "The Pazmanian Devil." In 1991, he broke his neck in a car accident. Doctors said he would never fight again, but Paz trained hard. He got back in the boxing ring and won even more world titles. He is very popular in his home state. Paz was born in Cranston.

Cities

Providence is Rhode Island's capital and largest city. It is also the state's oldest permanent settlement. Roger Williams founded the city in 1636 where the Providence River runs into Narragansett Bay. It became an important seaport and major industrial center. Today, Providence also has a strong service economy. There are large financial institutions and eight hospitals. Local colleges include Brown University and Rhode Island School of Design. The population of Providence is 172,459.

Newport was once a major port for American pirates and the slave trade. Today, the Naval War College, Naval Undersea Warfare Center, and a training center are located at Newport's naval station. The city is famous for its beautiful mansions. Presidents John F. Kennedy and Dwight Eisenhower were frequent visitors. Newport's population is 25,359.

A famous National Recreation Trail known as "Cliff Walk" allows people to walk along the rugged ocean shore and see Newport's beautiful mansions.

Pawtucket is the birthplace of America's Industrial Revolution. It was here Samuel Slater built the first American cotton-spinning mill that used waterpower in 1790. The city still makes textiles, jewelry, and silverware. There is also an active arts community. Pawtucket's population is 72,342.

Slater's Mill

Warwick is Rhode Island's second-largest city. The first blood of the American Revolution was spilled here in 1772, when the British ship *Gaspee* was attacked. The city today has retail centers, high technology industries, financial services, and tourism. Warwick's population is 85,097.

Pontiac Mills

Transportation

Rhode Island's largest commercial airport is T.F. Green Airport in Warwick. It services more than 5 million passengers every year. Other airports include Block Island State Airport and Westerly State Airport.

Amtrak's Acela Express and Acela Regional pass through the state. Reaching speeds of 150  miles per hour (241 km/hr), the Acela Express runs from Boston to Washington, D.C. The Providence and Worcester Railroad Company provides freight services.

Passenger ferries go to Block Island and Martha's Vineyard. Others connect Providence, Newport, and Jamestown. The deep-water harbor at Providence has domestic and international shipping. It handles more than 9 million tons (8.2 million metric tons) of asphalt, cement, fuel, salt, scrap metal, and other cargo.

Interstate I-95 goes through the state from the southwest to the northeast. Rhode Island has about 3,000 miles (4,828 km) of roads and 836 bridges.

The Claiborne Pell Newport Bridge crosses the Narragansett Bay, connecting the city of Newport on Aquidneck Island with the town of Jamestown on Conanicut Island.

Natural Resources

Commercial fishing is a Rhode Island tradition. Millions of pounds of cod, flounder, hake, haddock, whiting, and other fish are caught. Lobster is also caught.

Fish farming produces more than one million dollars worth of oysters and clams. Oysters have been commercially raised in the state since 1798.

There are 850 farms in Rhode Island. Their average size is 71 acres (29 ha). Their main income is from greenhouse and nursery plants, dairy, corn, and potatoes. The state's total agricultural output is worth about $65 million.

Rhode Island has 385,000 acres (155,804 ha) of forest, which is about 60 percent of the state's land area. Millions of feet of lumber products are produced every year.

A quahog fisherman working in Narragansett Bay. Quahogs are large clams with hard, round shells found on the Atlantic Coast of North America. They are good to eat and are often used in clam chowder and other foods made with clams.

Industry

Samuel Slater built the first water-powered cotton mill at Pawtucket in 1790. It started America's Industrial Revolution. Rhode Island became a major manufacturing center in the early 1800s.

The state continues to manufacture textiles. Other products include boats, computers, chemicals, electronics, instruments, plastics, and metal products.

There are many well-known businesses in Rhode Island. Among them is Hasbro, which is one of the world's biggest toy companies. Among its most popular toys is Mr. Potato Head, and the board game Monopoly.

Hasbro is in Pawtucket, Rhode Island.

Other Rhode Island companies include CVS Caremark, the nation's largest drugstore chain, and Textron, the maker of Bell helicopters and Cessna airplanes. There are also major health care, insurance, and financial service companies.

Tourism is important to Rhode Island's economy. Its impact on the state's economy is $2.26 billion. Tourism employs nearly 39,000 people.

Many tourists visit Rhode Island each year.

Sports

Sailing has always been a major activity in Rhode Island. The America's Cup yacht races were held at Newport from 1930 to 1983. Some of these vintage sailboats are still in the state, including the famous *Courageous*. It

The *Courageous* won the 1977 America's Cup yacht race.

became Rhode Island's official yacht in 1997.

Other popular water-related activities include motor boating, diving, canoeing, diving, kayaking, and sport fishing. Some people just like to build sand castles. There are more than 100 swimming beaches.

People camp and hike in the state's beautiful woods and along the scenic seashore. There is bicycling, bird watching, horseback riding, and motorcycling. The state has many fine golf courses. About seven percent of the state's land area is open to hunting.

The Women's U.S. Open was held at the Newport Country Club in 2006.

Entertainment

Rhode Island has many festivals, fairs, and museums. Its attractions include lighthouses, carousels, airplanes, and mansions. The Newport Jazz Festival features world-famous jazz musicians and singers.

Sailing-related exhibits are found at the Herreshoff Marine Museum, Museum of Yachting, and Naval War College Museum. There are also many popular sailboat races, events, and shows.

An Oracle aerobatics biplane flies past a yacht. The yacht competed in the America's Cup, while the plane competed in the popular Rhode Island National Guard Air Show.

The International Tennis Hall of Fame Museum is at Newport, where the first American tennis tournament took place in 1881. The museum's collection includes 100,000 photos, 1,000 movies, and 15,000 objects.

The Roger Williams Park Zoo in Providence is the third oldest in the nation. Founded in 1872, the zoo is one of the best in New England. It has about 700,000 visitors each year.

A polar bear takes a swim at his home in the Roger Williams Park Zoo in Providence, Rhode Island. The zoo is the third oldest in the nation.

Timeline

1524—Italian explorer Giovanni de Verrazzano reaches Rhode Island.

1614—Adriaen Block and John Smith survey the Rhode Island area.

1636—Roger Williams founds the city of Providence.

1663—Rhode Island becomes a British colony.

1675-1676—King Philip's War. Many colonists and Native Americans die before the colonists win.

 **1772**—The first blood of the American Revolution is spilled when patriots burn the English ship HMS *Gaspee* in Narragansett Bay.

 **1787**—Rhode Island bans slave trade.

 **1790**—Rhode Island ratifies the U.S. Constitution to become the 13th state. The first water-powered cotton mill is built by Samuel Slater.

 **1861-1865**—Rhode Islanders serve in the Civil War, staying with the Union.

 **1945-Modern Day**—Rhode Island's economy goes from manufacturing to service and tourism.

Glossary

America's Cup—The most prestigious trophy awarded in the sport of sailing. It attracts top sailors and yacht designers. Sailors have competed for the America's Cup for more than 150 years.

Continental Plate—Large, continent-sized pieces of Earth's crust, which move over millions of years. When plates collide, mountain ranges are pushed upward.

Estuary—The mouth of a large river, where the tide meets the flowing water.

Glacier—Huge ice shields that grow and shrink when the climate changes. They shape the land beneath them.

Industrial Revolution—Advances in machine technology, especially in steam power, iron-making, and textiles. The world's economies started relying more on manufacturing instead of farming and manual labor.

Moraine—A large pile of silt, soil, and rocks left behind by a melted glacier. The deposits usually make good farmland.

Pirate—A criminal who commits acts of robbery, murder, or kidnapping by attacking merchant ships.

Privateer—A privately owned ship that has a government license to attack and capture enemy vessels. The government is a partner, and shares in the profits.

Revolutionary War—The war fought between the American colonies and Great Britain from 1775-1783. It is also known as the War of Independence or the American Revolution.

Storm Surge—When hurricane winds push the ocean's water up on land. The rise in the water level can be more than 25 feet (8 m), and may flood low-lying islands, cities, and farms. Storm surges can be deadly.

Underground Railroad—Not a real railroad, but a network of safe houses and transportation that helped slaves escape into northern states or Canada.

Index